MONIQUE REID

The Prayers of a
WARRIOR QUEEN

30
DAY WOMEN'S GUIDE
TO EFFECTIVELY USE
YOUR WEAPON OF PRAYER
TO WAGE WAR ON THE ENEMY

The Prayers of a Warrior Queen

Special Thanks and Dedication

I would like to dedicate this book to our Heavenly Father for creating us, to Jesus Christ for dying and defeating death so that we would have life after death, and to the Holy Spirit for leading and guiding me through this process, and in life. I would like to give a special thanks to my husband, Uzziah Reid, for supporting me on this journey and for putting in as much work as I have. I love you, Papi!

I would like to thank my mother, Carmen Swanigan, a beautiful and strong woman of God, who raised me and loved me even when I was hard-headed and difficult to love. I am so thankful to God for you. I love you, Mommy! Thank you to my Abuela Carmen Ramos, a mighty woman of God and the Queen of the family. Te amo Abuela! I would like to thank all the women in my family for your continual support and for loving me through the hard times and teaching me. My family is the definition of "Ride or Die". I want to give thanks to my Apostle Gigi Palmer for being a true woman of God and for being obedient and humble to say what God has spoken, no matter what it is. I love you, Apostle!

I dedicate this book to my children A.J., Hope, and Faith. God gave me the strength to survive so that I could make sure you guys have a better life than I did! Besides God, you guys are the reason that I kept moving. I had you guys on my mind while I was going through all the tough times. I did it for you because I love you with all my heart! Mommy loves you, babies!

Contents

BEFORE YOU BEGIN

Hello Warrior Queen! This prayer book is dedicated to you, the woman reading this. There is a reason why God placed it in your heart to invest in this book. The very breakthrough that you've been fighting for could be in your hands right now!

God led me to create something for women to empower them to break free from depression, low self-esteem, and low confidence for themselves. There were times when I was writing this book where the Holy Spirit was on me so heavily that I had to stop and cry out and worship. I pray that you also have a personal experience with the Holy Spirit while reading this. Sometimes, we tend to think we need someone to hold our hand while we are going through something or feeling down. The problem is that there will come a time when the one you always turn to in your time of need will not be there. What will you do then?

I went through depression by myself and had to fight to get out by myself. The reason is that I didn't know that I was in depression, so I couldn't talk about it. I knew I was overwhelmingly sad but couldn't show it because I'm a mom and I needed to be strong for my children, so I suffered alone. I wanted to be happy, and I made a lot of mistakes seeking out happiness until I decided that I was going to serve God for the rest of my life and I found my strength in Him to break free for myself.

I am reaching out to women who are struggling with the

same thing I was, and I want to help them avoid making the same mistakes and help them to break free for themselves quicker than it took for me. Most often, depression comes to take over you when you are by yourself, and that is the time that you are going to have to defeat it on your own.

I read a quote once that said, "Faith is the currency of heaven and prayer is the means by which we exchange sorrow for joy, ashes for beauty, and spiritual deadness for supernatural power!" Wow! Can you just imagine that the minute you begin to pray, the God of the universe splits heaven and moves mountains for you! Picture that, because that's exactly what He does when you have a consistent prayer life! Amazing, isn't it! God is waiting for you to build a bridge that leads to a relationship with Him so you can commune with Him at any time! That bridge is built by prayers, authentic prayers. Prayers that move Him, when you pray to Him in spirit and in truth. God wants you to seek Him, not for what He can do for you or only when you need help. No, God wants you to seek Him for who He is, out of love, out of a pure heart to create a relationship. Prayer is essential to survive this walk we call life! It is communication with our heavenly Father. I heard a preacher say, "Prayer is a divine summons that causes God to step into the affairs of men! Prayer overrides the adversary!"

I implore you, seek God, not for what you can gain materialistically, but for what you can gain spiritually: everlasting life, peace, joy, victory, salvation, and authority over the enemy! Make yourself a willing vessel that He can use at His will when someone needs a word of encouragement or prayer. This is seeking Him in spirit and truth. When you seek Him only for what He can do for you, you turn away after He gives it to you! You must give God your true worship and praise offering. Surrender to His will, and I promise you won't regret it! He's waiting for you to open the door to your heart, so He can enter into your life and begin to break off those things that have caused you so much pain and turmoil. He wants to break it off so He can remold you back to your original state, His image.

Now, if you are not saved, that's fine. This is the perfect time to invite God into your life and into your heart. It doesn't take for you to do anything special or even for a pastor or preacher to pray over you. You can obtain salvation right now, where ever you are! The Bible says in Romans 10:9, "If you confess with your mouth 'Jesus is Lord,' and believe in your heart that God raised Him from the dead, you will be saved." It's just a matter of the heart. Do you believe that Jesus is Lord and that God raised Him from the dead? If you answered, "Yes." Then, my sister, you are now saved by the grace of God! Praise God!!! You need to know that no matter what you've done in your life, how bad it was, how many bad decisions you've made, none of that matters now. Ask God to forgive you of your sins and He will wash you with the blood of Jesus Christ and you are now cleansed of all your sins! Praise God and welcome to the family!

Now that you are saved, the prayers that we will pray together over the next 30 days can be effective! The next step is to have faith that God is with you, even though you may not see Him or feel Him. Seek out a church home, where the Holy Spirit is not limited to flow how He needs to. Find a church that has loving leaders that want to see you grow spiritually. All these things don't come overnight, but you've taken a major step by accepting Jesus into your life! Now allow Him to cleanse you and work in you so that your light will shine before men!

WHAT IS A WARRIOR QUEEN?

You might be thinking to yourself, "What is a Warrior Queen?" Well, she is a woman who fights in this spiritual war against the enemy through prayer and fasting and the word of God with the authority that was given to her through Jesus Christ.

She obeys the word of God, and her leaders by living a Holy life. She does her best to do what is right based on how God has instructed us to live on this earth in His word, and if she makes a mistake, she repents and moves forward without guilt.

She believes God for what He said in His word and does not allow doubt to settle in her heart. She understands that once God has spoken, there is nothing else to do but believe Him for who He is and trust Him with all her heart. If God said it, that's it!

She worships God through her obedience, her sacrifices, her praise, her finances, but most importantly, with her heart. Your heart must be in the right place if you are going to fight in this war, otherwise, you're going to get hurt and could possibly hurt someone else.

She waits on God. This is very difficult even though it may not seem like a big deal. Many people fall short when it comes to this. We have to understand that we don't dictate when God moves, period. God will move in His perfect timing, and the best thing for us to do is wait and worship.

She loves with the love of God. Jeremiah 31:3 says, "…therefore, with lovingkindness have I drawn thee." (KJV) She understands that love is one of the most powerful weapons, aside from prayer and the word of God. Sometimes, love is all that is needed to defeat the enemy and save someone from destruction. God is love.

In short, she's pretty much like a woman version of King David.

Now imagine all those characteristics inside of you! That's who you are! A Warrior Queen!

1 Thessalonians

5:17

Pray without

Ceasing

READER'S INSTRUCTIONS

The power of life and death lye in your tongue! So, when you pray and use the word of God, you become a dangerous and fierce weapon to the enemy! With that being said, this cannot be taken lightly! Hear me, Warrior Queen! You have been placed on this earth as a vessel for God to use at His will. Prayer is how we receive our assignments, His instructions, our breakthroughs, healings, miracles, and so much more! Prayer is a weapon and when paired with the Word of God and throw in your faith, you now become a weapon of mass destruction to the kingdom of Satan, and, in the same token, a stone used to rebuild what was once torn down by the enemy! When you read these prayers, don't just read them; believe them! Exercise your faith and trust that God hears his daughter crying out to Him!

There are 30 days and each day has a different topic. Each day is broken down into a guide. First, there is my prayer for that day. Then, there is a scripture in relation to the topic of that day. This is meant to help you get into a habit of reading your word every day, read the entire chapter so you can get a full understanding of what was taking place.

Next, you will see a song to meditate on in conjunction with the topic. These songs are meant to help lead you into worship and praise, apart from a few towards the end. Listen to the lyrics and let them penetrate your soul.

You will then find words of encouragement. The purpose is for you to understand that you can and will do or be whatever the topic is. You are meant to say these words of encouragement with power and authority and believe that what you are speaking over yourself really does apply to you! Even if those words may not be accurate to where your life is at that moment, speak it into existence!

After you have read my prayer, read the word and fed your soul, meditated on a song to worship, and empowered yourself, you are now pumped and primed to go into prayer for yourself. You will see specific questions that are relevant to the topic for that day for you to answer and use if your prayer so that you can pray specifically. This is so you can have a structured prayer, and you know exactly what you are going to God for. Now, you don't have to limit yourself to only that topic, of course. Think of it more as a guide.

Finally, at the end of each day in the book, you will notice a specific saying: "Now, go forth and conquer the day Warrior Queen!" This is not just a saying. It is a charge, an instruction. You have read your word, worshipped, encouraged yourself, and prayed! You are now ready for battle! You are instructed to go out and conquer your day! Use what you've learned to fight against the attacks of the enemy that comes against you! These prayers are not only for when something happens. It would be best to use these prayers as preventative measures. The attacks are coming anyway, so you might as well prepare yourself and keep them at bay with your prayers. Just picture yourself:

A woman standing in the middle of a battlefield. The enemy is in front of you and everything and everyone that you love and hold dear is behind you. You are the only thing standing in between them and the enemy. You have a sword in one hand which is the word, and another sword in the other hand which is your prayer. The enemy advances at you and everything behind you. You raise up your swords and bring them down on the head of the enemy stopping him dead in his tracks. When the war has quieted, you retreat to your castle, sit on your throne, and continue to reign as Queen. This is who you are, a mighty woman of God who fights and reigns!

Now, go forth and conquer!

DAY 1 – MY PRAYER FOR TODAY: FORGIVENESS

Father, thank You for this day! Thank You for waking me up and keeping me in my right mind. Thank You for Your saving grace that continues to save me from everything that was sent to harm me, and even from myself. Please forgive me for anything that I have done that was not pleasing to You, knowingly or unknowingly, and give me the strength to make the decision to quickly forgive those that offend me. Today, I have made up in my mind to forgive all those that hurt me physically and emotionally, betrayed me, cheated on me, let me down, turned their back on me, talked about me, lied on me, misused me, and soiled my name. I know that if I don't forgive them for what they did to me, You will not forgive me of my sins. And God, I NEED your forgiveness! Thank You for Your forgiveness and for casting my sins into the depths of the sea, never to taunt me again! I praise Your name, not only for what You've done for me but, Father, for who You are! You are a great God and a good, good Father! I would never be able to express my gratitude to You for not leaving me where I was! I love you, Father! In Jesus's name. Amen.

Scripture of the day: Mark 11:25, 26 – *"And whenever you stand praying, if you have anything against anyone, forgive him, so that your Father in heaven will also forgive you your wrongdoing. But if you don't forgive, neither will your Father in heaven forgive your wrongdoing."* **(Read the entire chapter)**

Meditate on this song today: *"A Heart That Forgives"* by Kevin LeVar

Words of encouragement. **Look at yourself in the mirror and say with power:** I forgive (person's name) for (state the situation). I forgive myself for letting myself down and not loving myself the way I deserved to be loved. I am strong enough to forgive AND forget! Father, please forgive me for my sins and make me whole. Father, thank You for forgiving me! I am free!

What is your prayer for today? Be specific. Who do you need God to give you the strength to forgive? What do you need God to forgive you of? Now, pray that prayer in faith. Know that whatever you say in prayer, when you believe, you will receive! (Matthew 21:22 and Mark 11:24)

_____

_____

_____

_____

_____

_____

_____

_____

_____

_____

_____

_____

_____

_____

_____

_____

_____

_____

_____

_____

_____

_____

NOW, GO FORTH AND CONQUER THE DAY WARRIOR QUEEN!

DAY 2 – MY PRAYER FOR TODAY: WORSHIP

God, You are worthy of ALL the praise, glory, and honor! I bless Your great name! I will worship You forever! I will forever stay at Your feet and before Your throne! You created me to worship and I will do just that! I give unto You my sacrifice of praise! I must sacrifice my fleshly desires and push through to get into my true worship. Only then will the chains fall off, and the shackles come loose. This is where the enemy cannot find me because I am hidden in Your secret place. I offer up my worship and pray that it is a sweet-smelling savor before Your nostrils! I give all of me to You, Lord God because You have given me Your best! You are the beginning and the end. All things work in You, through You, and for You. I want to be a vessel that You use continuously. I am willing and able! You said a true worshiper must worship You in spirit and in truth! God, I am here pouring out all my spirit that I may receive Your truth! Incline Your ear to me, oh God, that You would be pleased with my worship and offering of praise! I will worship You forever and always! In Jesus's name! Amen!

Scripture of the day: Psalms 96:9 – *"Worship the Lord in the splendor of His holiness; tremble before Him, all the earth."* **(Read the entire chapter)**

Meditate on this song today: *"This Alter"* by Psalmist Raine

Words of encouragement: **Look at yourself in the mirror and say with power:** I was created to worship! No matter what I'm going through, I will never stop my worship! My worship is pleasing to God and it draws me nearer to Him! God loves my worship and I will not hold it back from Him! God deserves my worship! I will worship Him for the rest of my life!

What is your prayer for today? Be specific. Why do you worship God? Tell Him how deserving He is of your worship! Now, pray that prayer in faith. Know that whatever you say in prayer, when you believe, you will receive! (Matthew 21:22 and Mark 11:24)

_____
_____
_____
_____
_____
_____
_____
_____
_____
_____
_____
_____
_____
_____
_____
_____
_____
_____
_____
_____

NOW, GO FORTH AND CONQUER THE DAY
WARRIOR QUEEN!

DAY 3 – MY PRAYER FOR TODAY: DEPRESSION

I bind up the spirit of depression right now, in the name of Jesus! I break the power that it had over my mind right now! I will no longer walk around feeling less than. I will not be convinced that the world would be better without me! I am loved and treasured! Satan, I rebuke the lies that you have placed in my head and I plead the blood of Jesus Christ over my mind! I cast down every thought that has taken over my mind! I loose peace over my mind and my thoughts! I loose love for myself right now, in the name of Jesus! I am not defeated, and I am not worthless! I am special! I am fearfully and wonderfully made, in the mighty name of Jesus! God, You said You knew me when I was in my mother's womb and I don't believe that You wasted Your time making junk! I am a daughter of The King! I am of a royal priesthood, and I will carry myself and treat myself as such! I break the chains of bondage and yolk off my mind right now! Depression, I serve you notice NOW, in the name of Jesus! You have no permission to be in my life, my household, my mind, and my family! I cast you out! Go back into the pit of hell from where you came from, never to torment me again! I speak peace over my life right now! In Jesus's name! Amen!

Scripture of the day: Psalms 40:1, 2 – *"I waited patiently for the Lord, He turned to me and heard my cry for help. He brought me up from a desolate pit, out of the muddy clay, and set my feet upon a rock, making my steps secure."* **(Read the entire chapter)**

Meditate on this song today: *"You Say"* by Lauren Daigle

Words of encouragement. Look at yourself in the mirror and say with power: No longer will depression rule my life! No longer will I think of myself as less than what God made me to be! The world will be worse without me in it! I am fearfully and wonderfully made! I am worth love, marriage, children, happiness, and success! God said that I am loved by Him so I will love myself! I am stronger than I think I am! I have defeated depression! I have victory over low self-esteem! I have won against low confidence! I win!

What is your prayer for today? Be specific. What will you tell depression today? What do you say about depression ruling over your life? Will you break it today? It's your choice! Life AND death are in the power of the tongue! Now, pray that prayer in faith. Know that whatever you say in prayer, when you believe, you will receive! (Matthew 21:22 and Mark 11:24)

_____

_____

_____

_____

_____

_____

_____

_____

_____

_____

_____

_____

_____

_____

_____

_____

_____

_____

_____

_____

_____

_____

_____

_____

NOW, GO FORTH AND CONQUER THE DAY

Monique Reid

WARRIOR QUEEN!

DAY 4– MY PRAYER FOR TODAY: VICTORY

God, I thank You! I thank You for keeping me. So many times, my mind wanders, and I lose focus of what's in front of me and You always find subtle ways to remind me to adjust my lenses and get back focused on what I need to be working towards. You're such a loving God and I know where I would be if You hadn't sent Your Son to die on the cross for me. But God, it didn't stop there! Not only did Jesus Christ die so that I may live, but He didn't stay dead! He conquered the grave and death and through His victory, I am victorious! Thank You for making me victorious over every situation! Thank You for giving me the tools to fight against the enemy! Thank You for giving me victory over depression, fear, anxiety, unforgiveness, low self-esteem, low confidence, and death! Thank You for the victory over my enemies! I praise You in advance for the victory over my current situation, although I may not see it right now, I still praise You in advance! Thank You for the victory over the lives of my family! Thank You for victory over sickness! Thank You for victory over unbelief! I praise Your Holy name for You are worthy to be praised! I am no longer defeated! I am a champion! In Jesus's name! Amen!

Scripture of the day: 1 Corinthians 15:55-57 – *"Death, where is your victory? Death, where is your sting? Now the sting of death is sin, and the power of sin is the law. But thanks be to God, who gives us the Victory through our Lord Jesus Christ."* **(Read the entire chapter)**

Meditate on this song today: *"Victory"* by Tye Tribbett & G.A

Words of encouragement: Look at yourself in the mirror and say with power: I am victorious! I will live and not die! I have the power to overcome! I speak life over my situation, my mind, my finances, and my family! I am successful in all that I set forth to do! I win EVERY time!

What is your prayer for today? Be specific. What are you setting forth to conquer today? What are you proclaiming victory over today? Now, pray that prayer in faith. Know that whatever you say in prayer, when you believe, you will receive! (Matthew 21:22 and Mark 11:24)

_____

_____

_____

_____

_____

_____

_____

_____

_____

_____

_____

_____

_____

_____

_____

_____

_____

_____

_____

_____

_____

NOW, GO FORTH AND CONQUER THE DAY WARRIOR QUEEN!

DAY 5 – MY PRAYER FOR TODAY: FEAR AND ANXIETY

Lord, I thank You for Your grace. I plead the blood of Jesus Christ over my mind right now! I pray that You release Your angels that You have assigned to my life that they would be exactly where they need to be. I break the power of fear and anxiety over my life and mind right now in the name of Jesus! I bind up the spirit of fear, in the name of Jesus! I loose power, love, and sound mind, in the name of Jesus! I loose boldness, courage, and strength over my mind right now, in the name of Jesus, for you are a right now God! I know You hear me, Lord, and I thank You for inclining Your ear to me, oh God! I bless Your holy name, Father! I break the power of anxiety from making me feel as though I can't breathe, and I break that heavy pressure off my chest right now, in the name of Jesus! I will not have any more panic attacks! I bind up fear and anxiety and serve it notice now! I tell fear and anxiety that you have no hold over me! My mind and my body are off limits and you will not come nigh my dwelling any longer, in the name of Jesus! Now, Father, send a word of Your assignment for me on today now that I have broken fear and anxiety off my life. In the name of Jesus! Amen!

Scripture of the day: 2 Timothy 1:7 – *"For God has not given us the spirit of fearfulness, but one of power, love, and sound judgment."* **(Read the entire chapter)**

Meditate on this song today: *"The Break Up Song"* by Francesca Battistelli

Words of encouragement. **Look at yourself in the mirror and say with power:** I am not afraid of my past, present, or future! I have power over my situation, the love of God is in my heart, and a sound mind to make the best decision! I am strong, courageous, and bold! I will not fail!

What is your prayer for today? Be specific. What is causing you to fear? Call it out by name and break it! Now, pray that prayer in faith. Know that whatever you say in prayer, when you believe, you will receive! (Matthew 21:22 and Mark 11:24)

_____
_____
_____
_____
_____
_____
_____
_____
_____
_____
_____
_____
_____
_____
_____
_____
_____
_____
_____
_____
_____
_____

NOW, GO FORTH AND CONQUER THE DAY WARRIOR QUEEN!

DAY 6 – MY PRAYER FOR TODAY: CLARITY AND WISDOM

Lord God, thank You for saving me. Thank You for Your grace that is freely given. Wash away any unclean thing that lies within me. Create in me a clean heart and renew a right spirit within me. Father God, I clear my mind of all things that cause worry and stress and confusion. Father, You said if any man lacks wisdom, let him ask of the Lord and You will give it liberally. So, Father, I ask You for wisdom today. Give me the wisdom of heaven that I would be sure to always seek You first before making decisions and to be patient while I wait for Your answer. Father, I also ask for clarity in my life. Help me to see things clearly so I can apply the wisdom that You give me. Clarify, not only my natural thinking but my spiritual thinking as well. Help me to be wise in knowing that if I am unable to see something clearly, it could be a cloud sent by the enemy or that I just may need understanding. You also tell us in Your word, "In all thy getting, get understanding." Father, help me to understand that I must ask for wisdom to see things clearly in my life and in my purpose. In Jesus's name! Amen!

Scripture of the day: Proverbs 4:7 – *"Wisdom is supreme – so get wisdom. And whatever else you get, get understanding."*
(Read the entire chapter)

Meditate on this song today: *"You Still Love Me"* by Tasha Cobbs

Words of encouragement. Look at yourself in the mirror and say with power: I am a wise woman! I will seek the Lord for any decisions I make! I will be patient and wait for His answer. I have a clear mind to hear the Lord's instruction. There is no confusion in my camp! I am wise to obey the word of the Lord!

What is your prayer for today? Be specific. What situation do you need clarity and wisdom in? What do you need God to reveal to you about your situation? Ask God to give you wisdom liberally. Now, pray that prayer in faith. Know that whatever you say in prayer, when you believe, you will receive! (Matthew 21:22 and Mark 11:24)

_____

_____

_____

_____

_____

_____

_____

_____

_____

_____

_____

_____

_____

_____

_____

_____

_____

_____

_____

_____

NOW, GO FORTH AND CONQUER THE DAY

WARRIOR QUEEN!

DAY 7 – MY PRAYER FOR TODAY: COVERING

The Lord is my Shepard and I shall not want. Father God, You promised to keep me in Your wings and shield me with Your favor and love. God, I need You today to show Yourself great. Not that I would believe, but for your people to believe. I pray that the words that come out of my mouth are the words that You place in my belly. Lord let me be pleasing before Your sight and remove any flesh within me, in the name of Jesus! Let the women that you have sent for me to touch be receptive of Your grace, Your love, and Your salvation, in Jesus's name! Father cover me from the blows of the enemy that continually fly at me all day! Cover me from the curses that are sent to break me, destroy me, and kill me! Cover my family, Father, so that the enemy cannot reach them to try to get to me! Cover my babies from any hurt, harm or danger that is sent their way! Cover my husband and his mind from the attack of the enemy to try to cause division in our marriage! Cover my church family and the Apostle from all the attacks sent to cause division in the church! I bind up the spirit of division right now, in the name of Jesus, and break the power of Satan over EVERY area of my life and all those that are associated to me! I loose unity and love, in Jesus name! I loose the covering of God in my life and in my family's lives! In Jesus's name! Amen!

Scripture of the day: Psalms 91:4 – *"He will cover you with His feathers; you will take refuge under His wings. His faithfulness will be a protective shield."* **(Read the entire chapter)**

Meditate on this song today: *"You Covered Me"* by Dr. R.A Vernon & "The Word" Church Praise Team

Words of encouragement. Look at yourself in the mirror and say with power: I am beautiful! I am strong! I am worthy of love! I am a queen! I am an overcomer! I am fearfully and wonderfully made! God holds me in His hands, covers me under His wings, and surrounds me with His love! I will wipe my tears, get up from my bed of sorrow, and walk into my Queen hood! I got this!

What is your prayer for today? Be specific. What do you want God to do in your life? What do you need God to cover you from today? Now, pray that prayer in faith. Know that whatever you say in prayer, when you believe, you will receive! (Matthew 21:22 and Mark 11:24)

_____

_____

_____

_____

_____

_____

_____

_____

_____

_____

_____

_____

_____

_____

_____

_____

_____

_____

_____

_____

_____

NOW, GO FORTH AND CONQUER THE DAY

WARRIOR QUEEN!

DAY 8 – MY PRAYER FOR TODAY: AUTHORITY

Father God, You are my strength. In You I know that I will stand. You are where my help comes from. Help me to be a great woman of God. Help me to be a great mother and a great wife. Help me to be a great friend and a great influence on anyone that may be looking up to me, whether I know it or not. I know that without You I can do nothing, but with You, ALL things are possible. Thank You for the power and authority that You've given me! Help me to remember that as I go throughout my day, I have the authority to dictate how my day goes! I decree and declare that this is a wonderful day! I decree and declare increase in my life! I decree and declare health over my body! I decree and declare peace over my mind and peace all around me! I decree and declare supernatural favor, in the name of Jesus! I will walk in the authority given to me through Jesus Christ, and I will exercise it when the enemy tries to come at me! I rebuke the enemy from all the attacks he has planned for me on today and I cancel EVERY assignment right now, in the name of Jesus! Father, I thank you for the authority and for hearing my prayer. In Jesus's name! Amen.

Scripture of the day: Luke 10:19 – *"Look, I have given you the authority to trample on snakes and scorpions and over all the power of the enemy; nothing will ever harm you."* **(Read the entire chapter)**

Meditate on this song today: *"Authority"* by Karen Clark Sheard

Words of encouragement. **Look at yourself in the mirror and say with power:** I am strong in the Lord! He will hold me in His hands! I have power and authority to walk on snakes and scorpions! I have ALL power over the enemy and my situation! NOTHING will ever harm me! I will conquer this day and every day ahead of me! I will have an amazing day!

What is your prayer for today? Be specific. What do you take authority over today? What snakes and scorpions will you trample on today? Now, pray that prayer in faith. Know that whatever you say in prayer, when you believe, you will receive! (Matthew 21:22 and Mark 11:24)

_____

_____

_____

_____

_____

_____

_____

_____

_____

_____

_____

_____

_____

_____

_____

_____

_____

_____

_____

_____

_____

_____

_____

NOW, GO FORTH AND CONQUER THE DAY WARRIOR QUEEN!

DAY 9 - MY PRAYER FOR TODAY: BIND AND LOOSE

Lord, I lift Your name high above all other names! Your name is great! Your name is greater than all other names! Your name is greater than any stronghold that tries to grip me! Your name is greater than any bondage over my mind that tries to hinder me! I break the chains of bondage and strongholds over my life right now, in the name of Jesus, and I bind up the enemy from coming against me through my thoughts! I bind up the attack that was sent to me today, in the name of Jesus! I bind up the spirit of fear! I bind up the spirit of unbelief! I bind up double mindedness! I bind up pride, in the mighty name of Jesus! I bind up division! I bind up the lies of the enemy! I bind up every witch and warlock sent to kill me and my family, in the name of Jesus! I bind up the curses spoken against me and my family, in the matchless name of Jesus! I loose Your peace over my mind and over my household right now, in the name of Jesus! I loose Your power, God, in the name of Jesus! I loose Your freedom right now, in the name of Jesus! I loose Your Holy Spirit to move freely in my life and my family's lives! I loose Your protection from the enemy! I loose unity! I loose the blood of Jesus Christ to flow over me and my family, in Jesus's name! I loose truth over my tongue and my family's! I loose love, power, and sound mind! I loose boldness and courage! I loose humility! Lord God, thank You for hearing me and thank You for Your word! In Jesus's name!

Amen!

Scripture of the day: Matthew 18:18 – "*I assure you: Whatever you bind on earth is already bound in heaven, and whatever you loose on earth is already loosed in heaven.*" **(Read the entire chapter)**

Meditate on this song today: "*Break Every Chain*" by Tasha Cobbs

Word of encouragement: Look at yourself in the mirror and say with power: I am no longer bound by the enemy! I am overwhelming victorious! Never again will I allow the enemy to pull me back into captivity again! I loose myself from depression! I loose myself from feeling worthless! My joy is in the Lord and He will hold me up! God loves me, and I love myself too!

What is your prayer for today? Be specific. What do you need to break free from in your life? What needs to be bound up in your house, and what needs to be loosed? Now, pray that prayer in faith. Know that whatever you say in prayer, when you believe, you will receive! (Matthew 21:22 and Mark 11:24)

_____

_____

_____

_____

_____

_____

_____

_____

_____

_____

_____

_____

_____

_____

_____

_____

_____

_____

_____

_____

_____

NOW, GO FORTH AND CONQUER THE DAY

WARRIOR QUEEN!

DAY 10 – MY PRAYER FOR TODAY: THANKFULNESS

Lord, I want to thank You for the many blessings that You've given me! I thank You for my children, and for them being healthy. I thank You for a second chance at love and marriage. Thank You for being in my right mind and wanting to learn more of You! Thank You for the way that You created me! Thank You for my awesome family! Thank You for loving me when I couldn't even look at myself. Thank You for a job to pay tithes and bills and to be a blessing to others. Thank You for a place to live. Thank You for my vehicle. Thank You for food in my belly and clothes on my body. All these things we tend to take for granted and don't stop to say thank You for. God, thank You for the use of my limbs, movement in my body, sight, speech, breath in my lungs! I am so thankful that You take care of me and my family and ALL our needs. I give You praise in advance for the blessings that are on their way! In Jesus's name! Amen!

Scripture of the day: 1 Thessalonians 5:16-18 – *"Rejoice always! Pray consistently! Give thanks in everything, for this is God's will for you in Christ Jesus."* **(Read the entire chapter)**

Meditate on this song today: *"What Mercy Did For Me"* by Crystal Yates, Micah Tyler, Joshua Sherman

Words of encouragement. **Look at yourself in the mirror and say with power:** I may not have everything I want, yet, but God provides ALL my needs! I am blessed over and abundantly! My blessings will chase me down! My family is blessed and healthy! I am thankful for where God brought me from and is bringing me to! I am thankful for who God made me to be!

What is your prayer for today? Be specific. Why are you thankful to God? What are you thankful to God for, even before He blesses you with it? Giving Him praise for it before you see it shows your faith! Now, pray that prayer in faith. Know that whatever you say in prayer, when you believe, you will receive! (Matthew 21:22 and Mark 11:24)

_____

_____

_____

_____

_____

_____

_____

_____

_____

_____

_____

_____

_____

_____

_____

_____

_____

_____

_____

_____

Now, go forth and conquer the day Warrior Queen!

DAY 11 – MY PRAYER FOR TODAY: FAITH

God! Fill me up with faith that I will walk this thing out and NEVER faint! Increase my faith, oh God, that I would believe EVERYTHING that You say about me and what You have called me to do for Your kingdom on this earth and who You have called me to be! Provide the fire, Lord, that I would be the sacrifice. Father, I ask for the unshakable gift of faith! I want my faith to be as a sword that I thrust into the ground so when the winds and storms of life blow, though my feet may lift from the ground if I hold onto that sword, I will not be moved! Lord, give me faith like a flaming arrow that is pointed at a target and released from the bow only to strike dead center! Increase my sensitivity to Your Holy Spirit that I would be able to immediately hear what You say and act without hesitation! In the name of Jesus! God let me be the stone that You use to rebuild what was torn down! Thank You for the faith of a thousand men that I will run into the enemy's camp without fear and destroy EVERYTHING that is unclean! In Jesus's name! Amen!

Scripture of the day: Matthew 21:21 – *"Jesus answered them, 'I assure you: If you have faith and do not doubt, you will not only do what was done to the fig tree, but even if you tell this mountain, 'Be lifted up and thrown into the sea,' it will be done..."* **(Read the entire chapter)**

Meditate on this song today: *"Trust In You"* by Lauren Daigle.

Words of encouragement. **Look at yourself in the mirror and say, with power:** Lord, grant me the gift of faith! I will speak to my situation and it will be made right! By faith, I will do what the Lord has called me to do, even if I don't understand! My faith is strong and grows stronger every day! I walk by faith and not by sight!

What is your prayer for today? Be specific. What area do you need God to increase your faith in? Do you believe that God can do it? The first step of your faith is believing God. Now, pray that prayer in faith. Know that whatever you say in prayer, when you believe, you will receive! (Matthew 21:22 and Mark 11:24)

_____
_____
_____
_____
_____
_____
_____
_____
_____
_____
_____
_____
_____
_____
_____
_____
_____
_____
_____
_____
_____

NOW, GO FORTH AND CONQUER THE DAY

WARRIOR QUEEN!

DAY 12 – MY PRAYER FOR TODAY: PURPOSE

Lord God, I lift up Your Holy name! I thank You for creating me! I know You've purposed me to be on this earth at this age of its existence for a specific purpose. Father reveal to me what that purpose is! I know you have called me to help empower, encourage, and uplift other women, but God, You are a big God! I know that you have purposed me for so much more! Help me to retrace my steps back into my past and see all the areas where the enemy tried to kill me, stop me, and tear me apart, yet, by Your grace, I'm still here. Help me to recognize those areas that are tender to my heart. Lead me, oh God, so that I will not stumble. You said a righteous man's steps are ordered by You, so God, wherever and whenever You tell me to step, I will be obedient and do so. Until then, I will wait on Your instruction and trust You in the process! In Jesus's name! Amen!

Scripture of the day: Isaiah 42:6 – "*I, Yahweh, have called You for a righteous purpose, and I will hold You by Your hand. I will keep You and appoint You to be a covenant for the people and a light to the nations, …*"

Meditate on this song today: "*I Am Who God Says I Am*" by Myron Butler & Levi

Words of encouragement. **Look at yourself in the mirror and say with power:** I am purposed to be here by God! I will carry out the purpose I was created for and God will hold me by my hand and He will not let me stumble! I have been appointed by God before time began! I will seek out my purpose and when I find it, I will not be afraid, and I will step out on faith, knowing that God will order my steps!

What is your prayer for today? Be specific. What have you gone through in your past that makes your heart ache when you see others going through? What is your testimony? That is normally a big clue of your purpose. Now, pray that prayer in faith. Know that whatever you say in prayer, when you believe, you will receive! (Matthew 21:22 and Mark 11:24)

_____

_____

_____

_____

_____

_____

_____

_____

_____

_____

_____

_____

_____

_____

_____

_____

_____

_____

_____

_____

Now, go forth and conquer the day Warrior Queen!

DAY 13 – MY PRAYER FOR TODAY: SUCCESS

Father, thank You for this beautiful day that You created. I thank You for being a good, good Father! Thank You for caring about me so much that You order my steps so I don't fall or stumble. I know that, if I follow Your directions, I will be successful in all that You have called me to do! I decree and declare success in every area of my life! I decree and declare success over my money and my business, in the name of Jesus! I decree and declare success over my ministry! I decree and declare success over everything I lay my hands on and every piece of land that my feet tread upon, in the name of Jesus! I decree and declare success in my marriage and all that we set out to accomplish! I decree and declare success over the lives of my children! I decree and declare success over my plans for my future! I decree and declare that no weapon formed against me to stop me will prosper! In Jesus's name! Amen!

Scripture of the day: Joshua 1:8 – *"This book of instruction must not depart from your mouth; you are to recite it day and night so that you may carefully observe everything written in it. For then you will prosper and succeed in whatever you do."* **(Read the entire chapter)**

Meditate on this song today: *"Greater is Coming"* by Jekalyn Carr

Words of encouragement. **Look at yourself in the mirror and say with power:** I am successful in ALL that I do! With God ordering my steps, I will not fail! I am worthy of success because God said so! I am successful as a woman and I will walk in my success today and every day! I will not dwell on my failures because they couldn't hold me back then and they won't hold me back now!

What is your prayer for today? Be specific. What are your plans for your future? What are your plans for today?

Ask God to order your steps and seek Him for the directions so that you are successful in all that you do. Now, pray that prayer in faith. Know that whatever you say in prayer, when you believe, you will receive! (Matthew 21:22 and Mark 11:24)

_____

_____

_____

_____

_____

_____

_____

_____

_____

_____

_____

_____

_____

_____

_____

_____

_____

_____

_____

_____

Now, go forth and conquer the day Warrior Queen!

Day 14 – My prayer for today: Command Your Day

Father God, in the name of Jesus, I command my day to be incredible! I decree and declare that it will be an amazing day! I decree and declare that everything I set forth to accomplish on today will be done! I decree that I will not be stressed out or overwhelmed! Father, give me the strength to complete the assignments that You have given me on today! I command boldness to come forth, in the name of Jesus! I command mountains to be moved, in the name of Jesus! I rebuke the enemy from coming against my plans for today! I bind up every attack of discourse, confusion, forgetfulness, slothfulness, and stress, in the name of Jesus! I loose peace, promptness, positive energy, witty ideas and inventions, and a memory of an elephant, in the name of Jesus! This is the day that the Lord has made and, not only will I be glad in it, but I will be successful in it too! In Jesus's name, I pray! Amen!

Scripture of the day: Proverbs 18:20-21 – *"From the fruit of his mouth, a man's stomach is satisfied; he is filled with the product of his lips. Life and death are in the power of the tongue and those who love it will eat its fruit."* **(Read the entire chapter)**

Meditate on this song today: *"Praise Him in Advance"* by Marvin Sapp

Words of encouragement. **Look at yourself in the mirror and say, with power:** I decree and declare that today is a fantastic day! I decree and declare that today is a successful day! I decree and declare that today will not overtake me or cause me stress! I decree and declare that no weapon formed against me will prosper! I decree and declare that this week will be incredible!

What is your prayer for today? Be specific. How will you command your day? What do you want your day to be like? What will you speak into existence on today? Now, pray that prayer in faith. Know that whatever you say in prayer, when you believe, you will receive! (Matthew 21:22 and Mark 11:24)

_____
_____
_____
_____
_____
_____
_____
_____
_____
_____
_____
_____
_____
_____
_____
_____
_____
_____
_____
_____
_____
_____

Now, go forth and conquer the day Warrior Queen!

DAY 15 – MY PRAYER FOR TODAY: INCREASE

Father, thank You for Your many blessings. Thank You for Your gift of life. Thank You for the freedom to come before Your throne and commune with You. God, I call forth increase in EVERY area of my life: spiritual growth, health, wealth, businesses, children, marriage! In the name of Jesus! Father, You say to remind You of Your word and in Your word, You say that when we sow our tenth, You will open up the floodgates of heaven and pour out a blessing without measure! Father, I am a seed sower. I pay my tithes, I give offering, and I sow love seed. I sow my personal time into the ministry for kingdom work! Now, God, keep Your promise that You made to Your people and don't tarry! Open up the floodgates of heaven and let the blessings of increase pour down like a storm of blessings! I call forth the harvest of my sowing! I command increase to manifest right now, in the mighty name of Jesus! Father God, I thank You in advance, by faith, for the increase because You already spoke it, so it is already done. Now, God, I rebuke the devourer from eating up my harvest through inconveniences, medical bills, dental bills, vehicle breakdowns, forgetfulness to pay bills and having late fees, the irresponsibility of overspending, and not saving money for emergencies! I bind up the spiritual cankerworm from burrowing into the fruits of my labor and causing it to rot, in Jesus's name! I loose supernatural increase now, in the mighty name of Jesus Christ! Amen!

Scripture of the day: Malachi 3:10 – "...*Bring the full tenth into the storehouse so that there may be food in My house. Test Me in this way,*" says the *Lord of Hosts.* "*See if I will not open up the floodgates of heaven and pour out a blessing for you without measure...*" **(Read the entire chapter)**

Meditate on this song today: "*Bless Me (Prayer of Jabez)*" by Donald Lawrence & The Tri-City Singers

Words of encouragement. Look at yourself in the mirror and say, with power: I call forth increase in every area of my life! I decree and declare harvest time! I see the gates of heaven opening right now and my blessings are chasing me down! I am a Queen and I will live like one on this earth! I am under an open heaven!

What is your prayer for today? Be specific. What area of your life are you calling forth increase in? How big is your faith to believe that you are worth the blessings that God is waiting to pour out on you? Believe it, Queen! It's coming! Now, pray that prayer in faith. Know that whatever you say in prayer, when you believe, you will receive! (Matthew 21:22 and Mark 11:24)

_____

_____

_____

_____

_____

_____

_____

_____

_____

_____

_____

_____

_____

_____

_____

_____

_____

_____

NOW, GO FORTH AND CONQUER THE DAY

WARRIOR QUEEN!

DAY 16 – MY PRAYER FOR TODAY: WARFARE

I come against that attack of Satan right now, in the powerful name of Jesus! I plead the blood of Jesus over myself, my mind, my children, my husband, my marriage, my finances, my body and health, and all that belongs to me and is connected to me! Satan you lose! I win! There is no weapon formed in hell that will prosper over my life! God said that ALL THINGS work together for my good! Yes, even this attack that was thrown my way to cause me to stumble! I will not fail! In the name of Jesus! I am an overwhelming conqueror through Jesus Christ! I bind up every witch and warlock, every demonic thing, every evil power that rises up against me, RIGHT NOW IN THE MIGHTY NAME OF JESUS! I rebuke every curse that was sent my way, every evil seed that was planted in my mind or the minds of my children, and my husband! I tear down every tongue that rises up against me and my household right now! This situation will not cause me to question my God! God is in control of all things and because I have faith, I know that He will cause this to be another victory under my belt. This is all for His glory to show that He is God. I can hear Him ask me, "How much faith do you have in Me?" Faith without works is dead. I will not allow a situation to cause me to doubt my God! I loose the authority over the enemy in my life right now! I loose the Holy Spirit to move freely in my life and to have Your way in this situation, oh God! I loose peace and comfort over my mind! I worship You, Lord, even in the midst of the storm! In the name of Jesus! Amen!

Scripture of the day: 2 Corinthians 10:4 – "*… since the weapons of our warfare are not worldly, but are powerful through God for the demolition of strongholds. We demolish arguments…*" **(Read the entire chapter)**

Meditate on this song today: "*Let Your Power Fall*" by James Fortune & FIYA (feat. Zacardi Cortez)

Words of encouragement. **Look at yourself in the mirror and say with power:** I wield the Sword which is the Word of God and I will use it to tear down the enemy and build up God's people! I am an overcomer! When I cry out to God, He rescues me, quickly! I am a winner and I will defeat this enemy and claim victory over this situation! I will not be defeated no matter what is thrown my way!

What is your prayer for today? Be specific. What attack are you under today! Bind it up and claim your victory! Will you be the victim or the victor? Now, pray that prayer in faith. Know that whatever you say in prayer, when you believe, you will receive! (Matthew 21:22 and Mark 11:24)

_____

_____

_____

_____

_____

_____

_____

_____

_____

_____

_____

_____

_____

_____

_____

_____

_____

_____

_____

_____

_____

_____

NOW, GO FORTH AND CONQUER THE DAY

WARRIOR QUEEN!

DAY 17 – MY PRAYER FOR TODAY: PROTECTION

Lord God, I thank You for Your favor that surrounds me and shields me! Thank You for Your eternal protection! I thank You that You have assigned angels to my life that surround me and keep me safe as I drive, sleep, and go about my day! I ask that You release Your angels assigned to my life, my husband's life, my children's lives, and my family's lives to do what You have assigned them to do! Release our war angels, God, that they would strike down any enemy that is coming against us! Release Your guardian angels that they would surround us and spread their wings wide touching tips to tips to create a forcefield that the enemy cannot penetrate! Release Your ministering angels that they would walk with us throughout the day and continually whisper Your words into our ears as we go throughout our day, and as we sleep at night, let them bring us comfort when we are distraught! I thank You for loving me that much that You keep me from all hurt, harm, and danger. In Jesus's name! Amen!

Scripture of the day: Psalms 121:5-8 – *"The Lord protects you;*

the Lord is a shelter right by your side. The sun will not strike you by day or the moon by night. The Lord will protect you from all harm; He will protect your life. The Lord will protect your coming and going both now and forever." **(Read the entire chapter)**

Meditate on this song today: *"Oceans (Where Feet May Fail)"* by Hillsong United

Words of encouragement. Look at yourself in the mirror and say with power: I am shielded by God's grace and love! I have angels all around me! When the enemy tries to attack me or my family, I won't fear, for the Lord is my shelter! I walk in favor and I will not be harmed! I am held up by the hand of God and no demon or devil in hell can stop me!

What is your prayer for today? Be specific. What is the enemy throwing at you that You need God's protection from? What is it that is causing you to feel vulnerable? Now, pray that prayer in faith. Know that whatever you say in prayer, when you believe, you will receive! (Matthew 21:22 and Mark 11:24)

_____

_____

_____

_____

_____

_____

_____

_____

_____

_____

_____

_____

_____

_____

_____

_____

_____

_____

_____

_____

_____

_____

NOW, GO FORTH AND CONQUER THE DAY
WARRIOR QUEEN!

DAY 18 – MY PRAYER FOR TODAY: HEALING FROM SICKNESS

Father God, I ask that You forgive me for my sins that I have committed against You. Give me a clean heart and renew a right spirit within me, oh God. Father, I come against every sickness, disease, and cancer that is trying to come against me, my husband, my children, and our family right now in the name of Jesus! I rebuke every unclean spirit that is trying to plant sickness, disease, and cancer in our bodies and I bind up that sickness! I bind up that disease! I bind up that cancer, in the all-powerful name of Jesus! I denounce it right now! You have no authority over me, my husband, my children, or our family! You are defeated right now in the name of Jesus! I plead the blood of Jesus Christ against you - sickness, disease, and cancer! I pluck you up from wherever you have tried to take root in our minds or bodies, in the name of Jesus! I command you to loose AND leave our bodies and minds in the name of Jesus! You have no right or jurisdiction here! I send you back to where you came from NEVER to return in the name of Jesus! Now, God, I loose your healing power over me, my husband, my children, my children's children, and my family! I plead the blood of Jesus Christ over us right now from the crown of our heads, to the souls of our feet. You said in Your word that we shall lay hands on the sick and they will recover! So, Father, I lay hands over myself, my husband, my children, and my entire family, in the name of Jesus Christ! I decree and declare that we are made whole by the blood of the Lamb!

I give You praise for the victory even now before it has manifested itself naturally. I know that You have already caused it to be done because I know that You are a God that answers prayers and You said in Your word that the prayers of the righteous avails much. So, Lord, I thank You for the healing! In Jesus's name! Amen!

Scripture of the day: Mark 5:34 – "*'Daughter,' He said to her, 'your faith has made you well. Go in peace and be free from your affliction.'*" **(Read the entire chapter)**

Meditate on this song today: "*I Am*" by Jason Nelson

Words of encouragement. Look at yourself in the mirror and say with power: I am healed! I am whole! My entire family is healed and made whole! I will believe the report of the Lord above all others! No matter what it looks like, I will NOT give up faith! I am a walking miracle! Sickness, disease, and cancer cannot remain any longer!

What is your prayer for today? Be specific. What sickness, disease, or cancer is trying to come against you or your loved ones? Call it out by name and renounce it from you and your loved ones! How much faith do you have in the God of the universe? Now pray that prayer in faith. Know that whatever you say in prayer, when you believe, you will receive! (Matthew 21:22 and Mark 11:24)

_____

_____

_____

_____

_____

_____

_____

_____

_____

_____

_____

_____

_____

_____

_____

_____

_____

_____

_____

NOW, GO FORTH AND CONQUER THE DAY

WARRIOR QUEEN!

DAY 19 – MY PRAYER FOR TODAY: ANOINTING

Lord, I pray that You have Your way in my life! I submit my will to Your will for me. Please forgive me of the things I've done that were not pleasing in Your sight. Cleanse me and wash me with Your blood Jesus! God, I ask that You anoint me with Your Holy oil. Anoint my mouth that I would only speak Your words and tear down the walls of the enemy! Anoint my voice that when I sing, You can move through the sound waves and break the chains of captivity! Anoint my hands that they would do Your work and be forever successful in all that I lay them on. Anoint my feet that wherever I go, every time my feet hit the ground, it will be another footprint on Satan's face! I ask that You help me remain humble in this walk and I submit myself over to You. Lord take away any pride within me that would hinder or delay Your work! Thank You, God, for trusting me and using me as a vessel! In Jesus's name! Amen!

Scripture of the day: 1 John 2:20 – *"But you have an anointing from the Holy One, and all of you have knowledge".* **(Read the entire chapter)**

Meditate of this song today: *"Anointing"* by J Moss

Words of encouragement. **Look at yourself in the mirror and say with power:** I am an anointed vessel chosen by God to do His Kingdom work on this earth! I will complete the assignment that has been given to me because God has covered me with His anointing. I have the living God working in me and through me! I am trusted by God to do His work! I will remain pure, holy, and righteous so that I would be acceptable to God!

What is your prayer for today? Be specific. What has God anointed you to do for His Kingdom? Have you sought God and asked Him to anoint you for what you have been called to do? Now, pray that prayer in faith. Know that whatever you say in prayer, when you believe, you will receive! (Matthew 21:22 and Mark 11:24)

_____

_____

_____

_____

_____

_____

_____

_____

_____

_____

_____

_____

_____

_____

_____

_____

_____

_____

_____

NOW, GO FORTH AND CONQUER THE DAY WARRIOR QUEEN!

DAY 20 – MY PRAYER FOR TODAY: FAVOR

Father God, thank You for this day that You have blessed me with. This is the day that You have made, and I shall rejoice and be glad in it! I thank You for Your favor that You shed over me. Lord, surround me with Your heavenly favor. You have the heart of the king in Your hands and You turn it to and froe like the rivers. I pray that Your favor follows me wherever I go! I decree and declare that I will have unmerited favor with men so that I would be able to do what You have asked of me! I understand that You do not call those that are equipped but You equip those that You call, so, Father, equip me with Your favor in the name of Jesus! I decree that I walk in Your favor all the days of my life! I speak the favor of the Lord over my life, my husband's life, my children's lives, and my family's life, in the name of Jesus! Thank you for Your favor that goes ahead of me and prepares the path! In Jesus's name, I pray! Amen!

Scripture of the day: Psalms 5:12 - *"For You, Lord, bless the righteous one; You surround him with favor like a shield."* **(Read the entire chapter)**

Meditate on this song today: *"This Is My Season"* by William Murphy

Word of encouragement. **Look at yourself in the mirror and say with power:** I walk in the favor of the Lord. His favor surrounds me like a shield. He turns the heart of the king in my favor. I'm getting ready for overflow in every area of my life! I will begin to see the tables turn in my favor because God is walking with me!

What is your prayer for today? Be specific. What areas in your life are you believing God to turn in your favor today? Who are the earthly "kings" in your life that you need God to turn their hearts in your favor? Lift up your situation and their names to God and watch Him work! Now, pray that prayer in faith. Know that whatever you say in prayer, when you believe, you will receive! (Matthew 21:22 and Mark 11:24)

_____
_____
_____
_____
_____
_____
_____
_____
_____
_____
_____
_____
_____
_____
_____
_____
_____
_____
_____
_____

NOW, GO FORTH AND CONQUER THE DAY
WARRIOR QUEEN!

DAY 21 – MY PRAYER FOR TODAY: UNSAVED LOVED ONES

Father, I come before Your throne humbled. Please forgive me of any sins that I committed against You and wash me that I would be whiter than snow. Heavenly Father, I come to You interceding for my family. You know the names of every single one of them that are not following You and that doesn't even believe. Have mercy Father, for they know not what they do! Restore their souls to You, oh God. Show them that You are the true and living God and that every knee shall bow before You! I don't want any of the people I love to perish for eternity Father. I pray that You would soften their hearts that they would receive You in their lives. When someone comes to plant a seed, let it sink in deep, and send another to water, and, God, You increase! I bind up the hand of Satan right now in the name of Jesus from keeping my family hostage! I break every chain and shackle, in the mighty name of Jesus! I command that they are loose from the chains that they have been bound in for so many years. I come against the strongholds in their minds right now! I decree liberty and deliverance and salvation over every person in my family, in the name of Jesus! I believe that this is already coming to past! In Jesus's name! Amen!

Scripture of the day: Jeremiah 31:9 – *"They will come weeping, but I will bring them back with consolation. I will lead them to wadis filled with water by a smooth way where they will not stumble, for I am Israel's Father, and Ephraim is My firstborn."* **(Read the entire chapter)**

Meditate on this song today: *"Reckless Love"* by Cory Asbury

Words of encouragement. Look at yourself in the mirror and say with power: My children are saved! My spouse is saved! My parents are saved! My entire family is saved! My friends are saved! I will be a living example of salvation because God saved me!

What is your prayer for today? Be specific. Who needs salvation in your family or circle of friends; call out their names? Have you introduced them to Jesus? Now, pray that prayer in faith. Know that whatever you say in prayer, when you believe, you will receive! (Matthew 21:22 and Mark 11:24)

_____

_____

_____

_____

_____

_____

_____

_____

_____

_____

_____

_____

_____

_____

_____

_____

_____

_____

_____

_____

NOW, GO FORTH AND CONQUER THE DAY
WARRIOR QUEEN!

DAY 22 – MY PRAYER FOR TODAY: OWNERSHIP

Father God, I lift up my hands as a praise offering for the many blessings that You rain down on us! You bless us with the day, for Your word says that this is the day that You have made, and we shall rejoice and be glad in it! Thank You for ownership, God! Thank You in advance for the house, though we are still in an apartment now! I praise You in advance for the vehicles that are coming! I thank You in advance for the properties that we will own and use for income! I thank You in advance for the businesses that we are starting and will own! I thank You in advance for the success that we walk in every day! You said to me that everything I set forth to do in Your name, I will be successful, and I will not fail! So, Father God, I take You for Your word and ask that You give me the strategies! Give me the visions, in the name of Jesus! Father, let it ALL be for Your glory! I remove my flesh from wanting all credit of the accomplishments! I bind up the hand of the enemy from coming against my mind and trying to plant seeds of doubt and unbelief! I rebuke the thoughts of worthlessness and break the spirit of fear, in the matchless name of Jesus! I loose victory right now! I loose power and authority! I loose boldness and courage! I loose confidence in the Lord and in myself! I will not self-sabotage! I will not abort the mission! I will complete the task that is set before me and I will leave a legacy for my generations to come! In Jesus's name! Amen!

Scripture of the day: Amos 9:13 – *"Hear this! The days are coming – This is the Lord's declaration – when the plowman will overtake the reaper and the one who treads grapes, the sower of seed. The mountains will drip with sweet wine, and all the hills will flow with it."* **(Read the entire chapter)**

Meditate on this song for today: "I'm Getting Ready" by Tasha Cobbs Leonard feat. Nicki Minaj

Words of encouragement. **Look at yourself in the mirror and say with power:** I'm under an open heaven! The harvest is ripe and I'm ready to reap! I am the lender and not the borrower! I will possess the land that my feet tread upon! I will own all that my hands touch! I will not take ANY credit but give ALL the glory to God!

What is your prayer for today? Be specific. What do you desire to own? How many businesses are inside of you? Know that when you seek His Kingdom and all its righteousness, all these things will be added to you. Now, pray that prayer in faith. Know that whatever you say in prayer, when you believe, you will receive! (Matthew 21:22 and Mark 11:24)

_____

_____

_____

_____

_____

_____

_____

_____

_____

_____

_____

_____

_____

_____

_____

_____

_____

_____

_____

_____

NOW, GO FORTH AND CONQUER THE DAY WARRIOR QUEEN!

DAY 23 – MY PRAYER FOR TODAY: MY HUSBAND

Father, thank You for my husband. Thank You for bringing me to a man that loves You! Thank You for giving me to a man that treats me like a queen and treats my babies like princesses and a prince! Help me to honor him as he honors You, Lord. Help me speak sweetly to him, even when I am not in agreement with him. Help me build him up with my words and actions and love and NEVER to tear him down, no matter what! Give him the strength and direction to be the priest, the provider, and the protector over our family! I plead the blood of Jesus Christ over my marriage and my husband right now in the name of Jesus! Direct me on how to help him, reveal to me the areas where he is weak so I can build him up in prayer. Teach us to communicate and not fight. Teach us to war together against the enemy and not each other. Help us to recognize the enemy from afar off so we know what areas to cover. Help us to be offensive against the enemy and not wait until he attacks us. As iron sharpens iron, help us to sharpen one another! We are one! There is no mine and his! I bind up every attack of the enemy, in the name of Jesus! I bind up the spirit of lust from coming into our home and into our mind! I bind up the spirit of division, in the name of Jesus! I speak unity over us that fuses us together so tightly knit that there is no gap or crack found by the enemy to even try to place a wedge between us! I loose Your love, power, and sound mind! I loose clarity and oneness, in the name of Jesus! I loose passion for one another only! I loose the power of unity over us, in the name of Jesus! Amen!

Scripture for the day: Proverbs 5:18-19 (NIV) – *"May your fountain be blessed, and may you rejoice in the wife of your youth. A loving doe, a graceful dear – may her breasts satisfy you always, may you ever be intoxicated with her love."* **(Read the entire chapter)**

Meditate on this song today: *"I Found Love (Cindy's Song)"* by BeBe Winans

Words of encouragement. Look at yourself in the mirror and say with power: My marriage is (will be, if you're not married yet) successful! My marriage is strong! My husband is a mighty man of God! (If he's not saved, keep repeating this!) My husband is the priest, the provider, and the protector! I will speak sweetly to my husband! I will lift him up and support him! I will not put him down even if he makes a mistake! I will not allow ANYONE to speak negatively over my marriage or my husband! I will not speak any negativity over my marriage or my husband!

What is your prayer for today? Be specific. What areas do you need God to touch in your marriage? What areas do you need to lift up your husband in? What areas do you need to improve in? Now, pray that prayer in faith. Know that whatever you say in prayer, when you believe, you will receive! (Matthew 21:22 and Mark 11:24)

_____

_____

_____

_____

_____

_____

_____

_____

_____

_____

_____

_____

_____

_____

_____

_____

_____

_____

_____

_____

_____

NOW, GO FORTH AND CONQUER THE DAY

WARRIOR QUEEN!

DAY 24 – MY PRAYER FOR TODAY: AS A WIFE

Lord, thank You for my husband. Thank you for my role as his helpmate, friend, support, lover, covering, and so much more. Help me to continue to uplift him and encourage him. Let the words that flow out of my mouth from my heart be sweet like honey. I ask that you help me to be submissive and allow him to lead me and our family as he follows you. Help me to see him as Your child, as well, so that I would be careful not to hurt him as I hold his heart in my hands. Give me the strength to endure the rough times and give me the freedom to enjoy happy times. I bind up the enemy from coming against my thoughts and trying to plant mistrust in him! I cast down every lying tongue that rises up to make me pull away from him! I bind up the lie that I am not a good wife! Father, You told me years ago that You made me to be a capable wife! I release myself from any guilt or unforgiveness that I may be holding on to from my previous marriage so that I can grab onto the joy and the growth of this one! There is no divorce! I will be faithful! My breast will satisfy him always! Father, keep my eyes on You so that I would be the best wife to him that You created me to be! In Jesus's name! Amen!

Scripture of the day: Proverbs 31:10-12 – *"Who can find a capable wife? She is far more precious than jewels. The heart of her husband trusts in her, and he will not lack anything good. She rewards him with good, not evil, all the days of her life."* **(Read the entire chapter)**

Meditate on this song today: *"Bless The Broken Road"* by Selah (also sang by Rascal Flats but this is the woman's version)

Words of encouragement. Look at yourself in the mirror and say with power: I am (will be, if you're not married) a capable wife! I will uplift and encourage my husband! I will not put him down! I will cover him in prayer and love! I WILL forgive him quickly, and NOT hold any grudges! I will love him through all the trials and tribulations! I will not hold myself from him out of spite! I will NEVER put him before God!

What is your prayer for today? Be specific. Remove everyone out the picture and take an honest look at yourself. What area do you need God to strengthen you in as a wife? How can you be the best wife that God has created you to be? Now, pray that prayer in faith. Know that whatever you say in prayer, when you believe, you will receive! (Matthew 21:22 and Mark 11:24)

_____

_____

_____

_____

_____

_____

_____

_____

_____

_____

_____

_____

_____

_____

_____

_____

_____

_____

_____

_____

Now, go forth and conquer the day Warrior Queen!

Day 25 – My prayer for today: My Children

Lord, I thank You for my beautiful babies that You blessed me with! Thank You that they are healthy and smart and funny and well behaved! Thank You for protecting them when they are at school and daycare and when they are not with me. I know that You can keep them safer than I can! Thank You for creating them to be their own individual people that have their own identities! Thank You for blessing them with a heart that loves You! Father God, I know that they are only borrowed, and they truly belong to You, but thank You for the time that You allowed for me to hold them in my arms as babies. Thank You for the times that I am able to teach them. Thank You for the opportunities to play with them and even discipline them. Help me to raise them up in the way they should go and keep them close so that they will never depart from You when they are grown. I plead the blood of Jesus Christ over my children, right now, in Jesus's name! Protect them from any hurt harm or danger! I rebuke the hand of the enemy that tries to come against them and I bind up and cancel every attack sent their way! I break every generational curse that is from my lineage and from their father's, in the name of Jesus! I decree and declare that my children will never see the inside of a jail cell, in the name of Jesus! I decree and declare that they will never suffer from addiction to drugs or alcohol, in the name of Jesus! Though they may wander and experiment as they grow older, I decree and declare that they will not be able to get away with anything they try to do that is not safe or illegal or outside of Your will for them! I bind up premature death, in the mighty name of Jesus! I loose long life, in the name of Jesus! I decree and declare that they will always be reminded of who they are in Christ! I loose Your love and protection over them right now, in the name of Jesus! Amen!

Scripture for the day: Psalms 127:3-4 – *"Sons are indeed a heritage from the Lord, children, a reward. Like arrows in the hand of a warrior are the sons born in one's youth."* **(Read the entire chapter)**

Meditate on this song today: *"A Mother's Prayer"* by Celine Dion

Words of encouragement: Look at yourself in the mirror

and say with power: My children are (will be, if you don't have children yet) blessed! They are good children! I will not tell them they are anything less than a blessing straight from God! I will build them up in the word and they will not stray from the Lord! My children are safe even when they are not with me, for the Lord is holding them close! My children are special!

What is your prayer for today? Be specific. What are the names of your children? Call them by their names individually and cover them in prayer. Go to war on their behalf! If you don't have children, pray for your future children, or the children in your family! What do you want God to reveal to you about your children? Now, pray that prayer in faith. Know that whatever you say in prayer, when you believe, you will receive! (Matthew 21:22 and Mark 11:24)

_____

_____

_____

_____

_____

_____

_____

_____

_____

_____

_____

_____

_____

_____

_____

_____

_____

_____

NOW, GO FORTH AND CONQUER THE DAY WARRIOR QUEEN!

DAY 26 - MY PRAYER FOR TODAY: AS A MOTHER

Lord God, thank You for the gift of motherhood! Thank You for blessing me with these beautiful children! Now, Father, endow me with wisdom. Guide me to be the mother that You have created me to be. Give me strength to be patient. Give me discernment to know when something is not right, even if it is not spoken or obvious. Give me courage to rebuke anything that comes against them or even from them and in the same breath, loose love. Give me the strategies to teach and discipline them. Let Your Holy Spirit pull me back when I've stepped out of line and forgive me if I disobey. I rebuke the lies of Satan that come to bring regret! I bind up the feeling of failure! I have not, nor will I, fail as a mother! I have made mistakes, but I have learned and gained wisdom! I forgive myself for not being perfect and I release myself from the ideal image of the "perfect mom" that says I'm not good enough! I bind up the spirit of doubt that tries to point out all my flaws as a mother, where I failed them, what I could have done better when I could have been there more, what I should have shielded them from! I loose peace over my mind! I bind up that worrisome spirit that comes to bring anxiety! My children will live and not die! I will raise them up in the Lord, so they will never depart from Him, but I will also, with the Lord's help and strength, let them go to make their own testimonies when the time comes! I break the jaw of the enemy from trying to make me believe that I am not a good mother! I loose confidence over myself in knowing that I did my best and understanding that there is no perfect way of doing this! I thank You, Lord, for guiding me and for keeping me and them! In Jesus's name! Amen!

Scripture of the day: Proverbs 31:17 – *"She draws on her strength and reveals that her arms are strong."* **(Read the entire chapter)**

Meditate on this song today: *"Slow Down"* by Nichole Nordeman

Words of encouragement. **Look at yourself in the mirror and say with power:** I can do this! It's hard, but God would not have given this blessing to me if I couldn't handle it! I am a good mother! I forgive myself for the mistakes I've made and the ones I will make! I will always love them NO MATTER WHAT! I am strong enough to let them go when the time is right! I am well equipped to complete this assignment! I CAN DO THIS!

What is your prayer for today? Be specific. What are you struggling with as a mother? What area do you need guidance and endurance and strength in? Now, pray that prayer in faith. Know that whatever you say in prayer, when you believe, you will receive! (Matthew 21:22 and Mark 11:24)

_____

_____

_____

_____

_____

_____

_____

_____

_____

_____

_____

_____

_____

_____

_____

_____

_____

_____

_____

_____

_____

_____

Now, go forth and conquer the day Warrior Queen!

Day 27 – My prayer for today: As a Daughter

Father, thank You for giving me life through my parents! Please forgive me for my actions that were not pleasing to You! I forgive them of their mistakes and anything they did that hurt me. God, help me to be the best daughter that You made me to be to my parents! God, I thank You for providing for them so they could provide for me! Bless me, Lord, so that I can now be a blessing to them. I honor them for all the sacrifices they made for me! I lift them up to You now like they lifted me up to You back then. Give me a heart of giving, so that I can give love back to them. I bind up the enemy from trying to place a wedge between me and my parents and cause us to drift away from each other! I bind up any attack against my parents right now in the name of Jesus! I speak health over their bodies and peace over their minds. I decree wealth in their hands! No weapon formed against them shall prosper! I decree and declare continued growth in our relationship! I speak a shield of love around us for I know that love covers a multitude of sins. I ask that

You give me discernment on what to pray for them because they may not tell their daughter about what they are struggling with. I speak blessings over them and all around them. Shower them with Your favor, oh Lord! In Jesus's name! Amen!

Scripture of the day: Exodus 20:12 – *"Honor your father and your mother so that you may have a long life in the land that the Lord your God is giving to you."* **(Read the entire chapter)**

Meditate on this song today: *"Because You Loved Me"* by Celine Dion

Words of encouragement. Look at yourself in the mirror and say with power: I am good enough! I am a good daughter! I will honor my mother and father! I will be the daughter to them that I would want my daughter to be to me! I will love them and support them and pray for them! I will laugh with them and cry with them! I will forgive them, even if they don't apologize!

What is your prayer for today? Be specific. What are your parents' names? Call their names out in prayer! What do you want God to do in their lives? Now, pray that prayer in faith. Know that whatever you say in prayer, when you believe, you will receive! (Matthew 21:22 and Mark 11:24)

_____

_____

_____

_____

_____

_____

_____

_____

_____

_____

_____

_____

_____

_____

_____

_____

_____

_____

_____

_____

_____

NOW, GO FORTH AND CONQUER THE DAY WARRIOR QUEEN!

DAY 28 – MY PRAYER FOR TODAY: MY MOTHER

Lord God, thank You for my beautiful mother, Carmen! She is truly a blessing to me and my family! You made her to be such an amazing woman! I lift her up to You God to keep her, protect her, empower her! I speak long life and health and wealth over her now, in the name of Jesus! She will complete the assignment that You have called her to do on this earth! I rebuke the hand of the enemy from coming against her body, her mind, her finances, and her marriage in ANY WAY, in the name of Jesus! I decree and declare increase in EVERY area of her life! I decree and declare peace of mind and the joy of the Lord! I bind up the spirit of division that may try to creep into our relationship, and I loose love and unity! I bind up the spirit of fear over her life, and I loose power, sound mind, clarity, and courage in the name of Jesus! I bind up the attacks of the enemy that tries to cause car accidents, in the name of Jesus! I bind up every attack from the enemy! Father, I ask that You release the angels that You have assigned to her life to surround her! I decree that she walks in supernatural favor! I bind up every tongue that rises up against her and tries to cause her to trip, stumble or fall! I loose victory in ALL areas of her life and in EVERY battle! In Jesus's name! Amen!

Scripture of the day: Proverbs 31:28-29 – *'Her sons rise up and call her blessed. Her husband also praises her: "Many women are capable, but you surpass them all."'* **(Read the entire chapter)**

Meditate on this song today: *"Mom"* by Megan Trainer

Word of encouragement. Look at yourself in the mirror and say with power: I have the best mother in the world! She is a blessing from God and I will cherish her! She is beautiful and strong! I am who I am because she is who she is! I forgive her for the mistakes that she made! My love for her goes beyond any words can express! I will always honor her for the many sacrifices she made while she raised me!

What is your prayer for today? Be specific. When's the last time you thanked your mom and told her how much you love her and appreciate her? When is the last time you prayed with her? What sacrifices has your mother made for you that you can remember? What do you want God to do for your mother? Now, pray that prayer in faith. Know that whatever you say in prayer, when you believe, you will receive! (Matthew 21:22 and Mark 11:24)

_____

_____

_____

_____

_____

_____

_____

_____

_____

_____

_____

_____

_____

_____

_____

_____

_____

_____

Now, go forth and conquer the day Warrior Queen!

DAY 29 – MY PRAYER FOR TODAY: MY FATHER

Heavenly Father, thank You for my fathers Gregory and Tim that You blessed me with! My father Gregory, who lives in my heart, and my step-father Tim! I was blessed to have two fathers in my life! I thank You for the time that I had with my daddy, though it was short, it was impactful! I thank You for bringing a man into my mother's life that embraced me and my brother. I speak a blessing over him right now in the name of Jesus! I speak healing to his body and mind! I speak wealth and prosperity! I rebuke the hand of the enemy from trying to come against him! It was You who protected him, Father, from dying in that car accident! I thank You, Father, for shielding him, because the enemy was trying to kill him! You are a good, good Father and you've blessed me with two of your best! I decree and declare long life over him, right now in the name of Jesus! I decree peace over his mind! Give him the desires of his heart! I decree and declare peace in their marriage! I decree and declare a retirement that most people can only dream of! I speak life and strength to his body! I bind up every attack that was sent his way to causes him to trip up, stumble, or fall! I loose supernatural strength and wisdom to continue to lead his wife and family as he follows you! I speak love over him! I decree and declare that he walks in Your Favor! I ask that You release Your angels that You have assigned to his life; his guardian angels to protect and guide him, his war angels to tear out the tongues that rise up against him, and his ministering angels to surround him with Your word! In Jesus's name! Amen!

Scripture of the day: Luke 15:20 – *"So he got up and went to his father. But while the son was still a long way off, his father saw him and was filled with compassion. He ran, threw his arms around his neck, and kissed him."* **(Read the entire chapter)**

Meditate on this song today: *"Butterfly Kisses"* by Bob Carlisle

Words of encouragement. Look at yourself in the mirror and say with power: I forgive my father for EVERY pain he caused me, and I release him from ALL the mistakes he made! My father is an amazing man of God! I will honor him! He is the reason I am here today! I love my father, no matter what our past looks like, he's still my daddy!

What is your prayer for today? Be specific. When is the last time you told your father how proud of him you are? When is the last time you treated him out? What do you want God to do for your father? Now, pray that prayer in faith. Know that whatever you say in prayer, when you believe, you will receive! (Matthew 21:22 and Mark 11:24)

_____

_____

_____

_____

_____

_____

_____

_____

_____

_____

_____

_____

_____

_____

_____

_____

_____

_____

_____

_____

NOW, GO FORTH AND CONQUER THE DAY WARRIOR QUEEN!

DAY 30 – MY PRAYER FOR TODAY: GOD'S LOVE

Lord God, thank You for loving me! Thank You for sending Your son, Jesus Christ, to endure the lashes, the beating, the name-calling, the abuse, the hatred, the lies, the torment, the pain, and the cross for me! I take that personal! Every time Jesus may have wanted to give up, He thought of me and said, "I can't!" Every time He may have begun to regret it, He thought of me and said, "She's worth it!" Every time they struck Him with that whip, He said, "She's healed!" Every time they bruised Him, He said, "She's forgiven!" THANK YOU JESUS FOR NOT GIVING UP ON ME!!!!!! It was because of You submitting to the Father and giving up Your life so that I would have mine, that I am free to be who God created me to be! I thank You Lord for Your never-ending, unconditional, matchless love! I thank You for drenching me with Your love! Endow me with Your love! Lead me in love that I may lead others to Your love! You said in Your word that it was through love and kindness that You drew me, so Father, help me to be loving and kind to others, even when it's hard. Remind me of the magnitude of Your love when the enemy comes to tell me I am anything less than loved! I rebuke the hand of the enemy from coming against me to make me feel like I am not loved, or that I am unwanted! You told me over and over and over, and You've shown me over and over and over, that Your love has no limits! So, Lord, please forgive me of anything that was not pleasing to Your sight. Father help me to forgive others as You forgave me, quickly! Help me to love others like You loved me, unconditionally. Help me to be at peace with all men! In Jesus's name, I pray. Amen!

Scripture of the day: Jeremiah 31:3 – *"the Lord appeared to him from far away. I have loved you with an everlasting love; therefore, I have continued to extend faithful love to you."* **(Read the entire chapter)**

Meditate on this song today: *"You Know My Name"* by Tasha Cobbs Leonard ft. Jimi Cravity

Words of encouragement. Look at yourself in the mirror and say with power: God knows me by my name! God loves me with an everlasting love! I am shielded with the love of God and

NOTHING can separate me from it! I am a product of my Maker, if God is love then so am I!

What is your prayer for today? Be specific. What area in your life do you need God to shine His love on? Who in your life can you love on purpose today? Now, pray that prayer in faith. Know that whatever you say in prayer, when you believe, you will receive! (Matthew 21:22 and Mark 11:24)

_____

_____

_____

_____

_____

_____

_____

_____

_____

_____

_____

_____

_____

_____

_____

_____

_____

_____

_____

_____

_____

_____

_____

_____

Now, go forth and conquer the day Warrior Queen!

YOU HAVE COMPLETED THE ASSIGNMENT!

Warrior Queen! If you are reading this, then you have conquered the task that you set forth to do! Congratulations! Now, let's do a self-evaluation:

- Over the last 30 days, what changes in yourself have you noticed?

- What changes have taken place around you?

- What changes have you seen in your household?

- What changes have you seen in your spiritual growth?

- What changes have you seen in your prayer life?

- What changes have you seen in your daily activities?

Big difference from 30 days ago! That is the power of prayer! Prayer truly does change things!

Don't stop here! Continue to build up your prayer life and

build that bridge of communication with the Father. Watch God continue to elevate you spiritually and naturally! He's a God of increase, so expect things to begin to take a turn for the better! Amen!

Thank you so much for doing this, not only for yourself, but for those around you. You may not know it, but the world is watching! The word says in Romans 8:19, *"For the creation eagerly waits with anticipation for God's sons to be revealed."* There are others out there that we have been called to help! This is a step in the right direction!

THANK YOU!

I pray you were blessed by this prayer book. Be sure to watch out for the sequel coming soon! Learn how you can become a Warrior Queen! Visit: www.iamawarriorqueen.com

You will discover my blog, my library, the Warrior Queen boutique and more information about me.

Follow me on Facebook and Instagram to join the community of Warrior Queens!

You can connect with me: themakingofawarriorqueen@gmail.com

God bless you Warrior Queen! Go forth and conquer!

Love,

Monique Reid - The Warrior Queen

Made in the USA
Columbia, SC
24 October 2018